There is a Greeting as Well as a Parting
Melinda Wolf

There is a Greeting as Well as a Parting
©2017, Melinda Wolf
ISBN: 9781937806101
Big Wonderful Press, LLC
Brooklyn, NY

All Rights Reserved

Acknowledgements

Grateful acknowledgement is made to the editors of the following magazines in which some of these poems were first printed:
American Literary Review: "To Go There"
Anthology of Magazine Verse and Yearbook of American Poetry: "There is a Greeting as Well as a Parting"
Comstock Review: "The Language of Horseshoes"
Cooweescoowee: "Returning Home Without Remembering"
Intro 14: "To a Hunter"
Kalliope: A Journal of Women's Art: "A Gesture Across Miles"; "Marianne's Dream"
Mudfish 4: "Tonight"
New York Quarterly: "Making Our Way"
Outerbridge: "Unfamiliar Rooms"
Pig Iron Press: "A Stepmother's Dream"
Phi Kappa Phi Forum: "When You Are Afraid of the Dark"
South Coast Poetry Journal: "Born Henry"
The Cape Rock: "Losing Friends at the Tent Revival"; "There is a Greeting as Well as a Parting"; "Approaching Sound-Cross Village"

Contents

Returning Home Without Remembering 5
There is a Greeting as Well as a Parting 7
Closing Sale 8
When You are Afraid of the Dark 9
Making Our Way 11
Tonight 13
To Go There 14
Marianne's Dream 17
Procession 18
Losing Friends at the Tent Revival 19
Hanukkah at Our House 21
A Stepmother's Dream 24
To a Hunter 25
Born Henry 27
The Language of Horseshoes 29
A Gesture Across Miles 30
Approaching Sound-Cross Village 32
Unfamiliar Rooms 35

Returning Home Without Remembering

I consider my mother's memory,
the gravel of name, action, emotion—
"this is sadness"—
now and not then.

She wonders what to do all day.
She asks me to come over to help her.
I, too, am at a loss.
She has been gone a long time.

We decide to clean her closet.
I pull everything out, one by one.
She says my name
as though she didn't name me.

She whispers,
"I really like spending time with you."
All that's left is black: black shirts,
black skirts, black pants,
huddling together like strangers.

The space fills with shadow.
Together we have agreed to this.
My mother and I look
into each other's eyes to find
nothing resembles
what we had come to know.

Somewhere, on a shimmering, silver pond,
we skate together. The sun shines on the ice
and snow, our eyes water from the cold wind
as we round each turn.

My mother reaches out, tries to catch my hand,
smiling as though she knows
she's met me somewhere before.

There is a Greeting as Well as a Parting

On Bridge St., in the 90-degree heat,
I loll against the brick buildings
waiting for the hours to pass
on the bank clock.
I think of friends who knock once
then go away forever,
of embarrassed new lovers
who turn the bedroom light on
and look at a stranger's body:
it is too difficult to begin again.

But it is in that turn toward light
when, from all the stories we narrate
so well, we must choose those
that tell ourselves.

We wait, shuddering awake,
sheet pulled to our chins,
for the words, like fugitives,
to come out of hiding
so that we might tell, without end,
the story of our beginning
again and again.

Closing Sale

We who love you may come looking for you
moving through the desert beneath the poker face
of the moon, a warm wind shifting against us,
dust settling on our shoes.

We continue to believe all paths lead somewhere
even those beneath the slivers of shadows
cast by electrical lines, tuning forks humming
their variable weight of power
humming carni or grifter or father.

What did you do to reach so far past dignity
to be pushed onto the unequivocal
playing field of a Texas Desert
coins tossed after you should you find a phone
should you want to say, I'm going to change my life.

We have followed you this far though
you vanish as we come close,
disappearing over the horizon line,
a tumbleweed caught and lost in bramble
indistinguishable from what created it,
a word broken and silenced by grief.

Maybe to be hoodwinked is an act of grace
the sky just a lie anyway: a seduction of
shifting light, a place to look for the dead,
and the stars, transfixed by all those wishes.

When You are Afraid of the Dark

> — *For Mary, who hid beneath my coat on the Older Adult Unit*

When you are afraid of the dark,
the light switch wags its tongue
at you, the windows fill with water
and the ceiling, the sky's emissary,
exists only to impress you
with the degrees of darkness.

When you are afraid of the dark,
your dead husband pauses
in the doorway,
leaves stuck to the bottom of his shoes.

When you are afraid of the dark, Jesus blushes
from his frame on the wall beside you
in the rosy light of your beating heart,
and the crucifix is a flurry of birds
rising at once from the dividing line
between yes and no.

When you are afraid of the dark,
you know darkness
has only begun to warm up to you,
and morning is just an idea,
like love,
or faith.

When you are afraid of the dark
it is so dark shadows are lost,
blackness weighs like grief
on your chest and you would take
up any offer:
a nightlight, a searchlight,
the bones' dull white,
even the flickering sight
of a once young girl
gliding through
a house of mirrors.

Making Our Way

If everything is no,
no to lying on the grass
where slugs massage the moist ground,

No to the sandy shore where alewife lie
stinking in the sun, lined up
like dirty dull knives;

No to the hot summer air, like pulling flames
into the lung-flumes, and no to the rain
leaving worm-trails down the windows,

to the children who worry their way
into the big bed when the thunder and lightening
crack, and it sounds close as a clap

against the head of their beds;
if everything is no, no to the tallis,
to the Torah cradled in the Rebbe's thin arms,

to the children's crosses
on the steamy bathroom window, no to the offer
of a place to set aside

not all but some responsibility—
no to the myth, the fable, the legend,
the ancestor—

then only by feeling the love
that could free us from reading the world

so closely

will we make our way,
our little globes of quivering light
softening the edges of these dark woods.

Tonight

Even with the curtains closed,
the lights off, we are first voyeurs,
then exhibitionists—
our eyes, when they meet,
are like spare rooms with beds made up tight.
Yet we've done everything right.
We've bent the broad palm of sleep's bridge
backwards, leaving this time, this open space
between decisions—
but like wind through closed windows, like birds
trapped inside roofs,
we cannot settle anywhere comfortably.

To Go There

I look at Lake Michigan
and want to sail there,
bob out of sight,
travel on, disappear from the view
like a plane climbing
into the horizon
to some other country
or to some large city.
Then my three-year-old daughter
comes from the water
carrying the sword of a dead fish:
there is no way to get there,
nothing is there
but the parasailor attached
to its speedboat
skidding through the sky
like a busted balloon on a string.

As my daughter's third birthday ended,
she lay in her bed and cried,
"I want to go back there."
She learned nostalgia,
that same kind of longing
that she has for her scraped knees
to heal, be the way they were.
What she needs to know
is not that there is nothing before
or behind us, not even the blades of light
she moved through
to blow the gold glow from the candles,

but that there is only her,
and each year another birthday
passing before her eyes like magic.

What she needs to know is that to go there
is to walk into a neighbor's home,
to sit down at the white Formica table
and begin the endless worry.

Marianne's Dream

"Never mind. The self is the least of it."
                    --Galway Kinnell

I

This morning my legs are startled
on the kitchen floor by an onion skin
a snake's skin shed crackling beneath my heel.
The sun shines on the fish bowl by the window
where one fish has bloated and risen like a balloon;
its gills shudder each time a breeze stirs the water.
I reach for the net small as the ball of a thumb
and lift the fish, put it in my palm.
I imagine the angry rattling of its body
as it must've fought the water,
as it rose like a small gold sun.
I press it to my lips.
I have shown this small love.
Look at me, I have kissed this small fish.

II

Last night I heard the stout men
in my dream whisper as they rose,
"Clever woman, she wants us to know
she is loving so she boldly makes show
of kissing a fish!" and when I awoke
there was a bruise on the puff of my cheek
ugly as a swastika.

Procession

"O to be delivered from the rational
into the realm of pure song."
             --Theodore Roethke

I watch the gulls fish before night-fall;
the fish hang from their wet beaks.
My old neighbor, with her rake, scours
the shore-line as she does every day,
to even the sand.

We look up, see the gulls
like faint smiles in the sky.
She says she hears the gull songs
as catcalls of men not met in halls,
in rooms, in the grocery, their voices
rising and falling like the gulls'
as they dip and wind to clip the beat
from a fish tail.

As she looks at the hill where the trees
stoop further toward the lake, the cliff's girdle
of sand losing grip, the last light of day
exposes her face, pinched and wrinkled
as the leaves of a fern.

What she can't see is Lake Michigan
gathering the shore-sand in an expansive embrace,
carrying it to Milwaukee or to the middle
where no one depends on it.

Losing Friends at the Tent Revival

Fastened down unwillingly, it trembles,
it's hot in here, and maybe it's the fervor
of the afternoon, but I swear it wants to break loose,
shoot upward, pregnant with faith, joy,
and a thousand or more people.

The speaker's hair sticks to his forehead,
his cheekbones. He has to scream his story:
"And there was an old man, death-dew
on his forehead, one week left in his eyes,
but he came to the Lord and…"—
the wind catches the tent and cracks it like a whip;
the noise of the traffic outside rumbles
like the very stomach of the devil.

Outside, everything changes:
the day doesn't stand on such sturdy legs,
the leaves don't speak in understandable tongues,
the Great Book doesn't answer.
I suppose I'm damned, or just don't have it in me.

This is why my two closest friends have left me.

When up they go, chosen, I'll be shaking my fists
at the sky or waving goodbye as it closes;
I'll be left in time
with wings that grow together,
struggling with a metallic or muffled language,
with the average rainfall,

with the dimensions of my dwelling.

Hanukkah at Our House

Before we recited the blessing
and lit our first candle
against the dying light of December,
I insisted we plug in the Hanukkah bush.
Aglow with blue lights,
it lit up the corner of the family room
and the family photographs behind it.
I thought we looked dreamy
in the blue-lit pictures.
My brother, older, wiser, said we looked
pitched up from the bottom
of a very cold lake to the shore.

Each season, I pushed for blue lights
on the trees outside but had to settle
for the Hanukkah bush
and a miniature Christmas tree
with plastic pine needles and ornaments
on the nightstand in my room.
Each year, I imagined whispering to Santa
my Christmas wish:
that he steal down our chimney
and leave my father
the best box of Havana cigars
he could find.

Santa never did come.
Each December we lit the candles
and we didn't do it

against the dying light through the window
as the sun set so the neighbors
could look in and see the yellow glow
softening our faces.

We placed the menorah on the built-in bar
in the corner of the family room
and huddled around it.
My father whispered the blessing
like a secret,
my mother cupped her hand
around the quivering flame,
my brother and I waited to get our gelt,
then unwrapped the stiff gold foil
and let the chocolate melt slowly
in our mouths.

We ate until our throats burned
and our stomachs ached,
until the candles caved in
and burned down.

A Stepmother's Dream

My father couldn't move
in his bed that night.
The next morning he told me
she had spoken, in her sleep,
a language he knew he'd never hear again.
It rose from her, guttural,
mad vowels clamoring over one another.

I asked him, "Did she open her eyes?"
He couldn't see,
he couldn't look at her
until she got up and began whirling
in the center of the room.
I asked him, "Were her eyes open then?"
"Yes," he said, "But they weren't hers;
like the eyes of a marionette
they clicked open and shut."
I told him it must've been
that she spun in a dream backwards
until she was a woman who
gathered the finely patterned cloth
of a blanket around her
and unleashed her legs,
let go of the comfort
of a filled womb.
She heard her son, screaming into morning,
that vulnerable hour
when all noise is a personal calling.

To a Hunter

I have seen feathers burst apart
in the sky like petals of a white
carnation,
two yearlings and a buck down
from a mountain in Wyoming.

I have watched him pull the long ears
of a rabbit apart,
watched him kill a deer
and with an ax, split the bone
of its antlers,
watched him run his jackknife
over a fish like a bow on a violin,
and I've had to work to keep
from heaving as I've watched him punch
the belly of a dead pig hanging from its hooves
in the barn. From the open flap
of the pig's jaw, he pushed the knife in,
slipped it the length of the body,
breathing heavily as he sawed through the skin.

I have watched him watch my robe slip
from my shoulders to the floor,
waiting to wear my scalp over his heart
like a fish on a string, dangling down
in shallows.
I have turned my head to my shoulder
oblivious to the clack
of rib bones he snapped

like branches for a fire.

Born Henry

            I

Born jaundiced, born with a purple lake
on your temple, the map of your past,
born Henry, surrounded by a blue you'll remember
deeper than where you'll remember—
you'll see the sea, the sky, the blue hosiery
hanging on the line
and each will stir your pulse.

You'll imagine the haze is recanted
from some other life where you woke into a blue
room
and went out mornings to milk, to weed,
to watch your mother through the window
as she rolled dough out on the corner.

           II

You'll think that that life, idyllic, makes this life
of prevarications, of preambles, of pre-engagement
contracts, of wills and distilleries and rattling
dishes and lawns drying up in the summer
to a yellow not unlike yours at birth
seem, what is it, lawful, willful, not quite kind.

           III

As you lie in bed with your wife, your legs hugging
her buttocks, you shut your eyes so tightly
you see blue. Henry, blue is too easy.
It is someone else's life
and it is as blue as your own. Your life is here,
now, in this bed, with this woman.

The shine-flex
of her muscle-curve, her olive skin,
the white scar on her jawbone are enough
to contend with.
They are the lights in the village
that is your own.

The Language of Horseshoes

Our words are heavy
horseshoes, iron rainbows,
archways into dark tunnels—
these once spitting hot
iron rods brandished
into benevolence,
bent beyond recognition—
poor birds, the sand forgives
their heavy thuds,
the clang that much louder
in its solid silence.

A Gesture Across Miles

I

I have found fathers of friends,
fathers I have followed, fathers whose arms
I've fallen into.

I have cleared a path and from its boundaries
at nightfall I have seen chests of men
and have chosen this one
or that one who might have held me,
who might have been.

II

I have walked, then later,
sunk into a chair and said aloud,
"Perhaps my Father cannot see,
his eyes bluish, delicate as abalone,"
and I have seen you stumbling
kitchen to bedroom
without a cane, alone.
I have said, "Perhaps my father is deaf,"
and I've seen you sit motionless
in a room where talk rose and fell,
a mere reverberation reaching you,
meek as branches scratching
against screen windows.

III

This is how I have reconciled
your unanswered gesture:
I have rendered you fugitive,
clinging to a wall, leaning
against a pillar,
hiding in the shadow of a tree,
waiting now, waiting always,
for my greeting to motion you forward.
Father, the gesture won't be mine,
but there is alchemy in waiting.

Approaching Sound-Cross Village

"What is so holy about corn?"
she said as she loosened
and tightened her fingers
around the steering wheel,
her luncheon dress buckling
around her fleshy arms.
"You've outgrown all this.
There's nothing here
but the smell of manure,
dead moths in corners,
and field mice."

I want to say, 'but corn grows
mile after mile, trees rise like braille
into the hands of the sky,'
but she mouths words
from behind the closed car window,
honks once and is gone,
leaving nothing but an owl's sound
through the tunnel of leaf and limb.

I brush flour from my fingers,
walk to the window, lean out for the breeze.
Maybe there is nothing holy about corn:
the annoying silk of the husk on the kitchen floor;
the small, hunched skeletons of field mice
turning up everywhere.

Always eggs,

always milking,
always something ready for slaughtering,

I want to farm, to hunt,
I know,
to pluck chicken feathers
like white daisy petals,
to pry the jaws of a fish open,
unleash the hook,
slit the belly,
wait in a blind at 5:00 A.M.
for the geese to pass overhead.

These interminable acres—
the rest of deafness must wait
to spin the body a web.
Really, it must be my mistake. So many
like me with love dark and small
as the crook of a knee.

Unfamiliar Rooms

How should we begin that moment after
her body shrinks,
her darkness less as it spreads
like a robe around the earth?
Should we sail on Lake Michigan
that very afternoon, raise the mast
like a marker over the water,
or box her clothes and jewelry,
lift the medicine bottles
and with a wet rag rinse circle
after circle off the nightstand?
The I.V., should we wheel it into the closet,
or will its parts protrude like limbs
into the sleeves of Father's suit coats?
What would she have us do?
Stand and look at the empty bed,
wait for her silence to pull us
into the space she inhabited,
that great gap like an unknown country?
Or would she have us lift a toast
to our loss of room after room,
to the corners of unfamiliar rooms?

www.ingramcontent.com/pod-product-compliance
Lightning Source LLC
Chambersburg PA
CBHW071550080526
44588CB00011B/1859